Insider's Guide to Attracting
Private Money

Insider's Guide to Attracting Private Money

By Mark Hanf

Dedication

To my father, Horst Hanf, one of the last of the breed of old-school businessmen who regularly made million dollar deals on a handshake. He taught me the fundamental importance of integrity and authenticity in all my business affairs.

Acknowledgements

My work in this endeavor, including this book and its accompanying video training program, has been possible thanks to the support and assistance of several individuals and organizations. First and foremost, I would like to thank my wife, Lisa, who has been my biggest supporter and who helped manage this project; and my two daughters, Kimberly and Christina, who are the brightest lights in my life. You are my inspiration.

I would also like express my sincere appreciation to Marcus Okun for his expertise in videography as well as his invaluable contribution to building the online marketing platform, and to the Marin School of the Arts Film and Video Department for the use of professional video equipment and state-of-the-art broadcast facilities.

Special thanks go to Helen Chang and the Author Bridge Media team for literary guidance and editorial assistance, and to Everett O'Keefe of The Solution Machine for publication, online platform and social media consulting.

GET YOUR

ATTRACTING PRIVATE MONEY
BONUS!

Exclusive Interview
with Mark Hanf

- Available only to book buyers!
- Discover how to find investors who want to invest their money with you!
- Learn about credibility packages and how to leverage them to close new deals

3 WAYS TO GET THIS!

BY WEB: Visit www.AttractingPrivateMoneyBook.com/bonus
BY TEXT: Text your name and email to (415) 779-7276.
BY PHONE: Call (415) 779-7276 and leave your name and email

(Standard message and data rates apply. Text HELP for help and STOP to quit)

Table of Contents

"You're just one relationship away from an explosion in your business"

—Robert Helms of *The Real Estate Guys Radio Show*

Introduction

Your Capital Opportunity

You have a ton of real estate knowledge. Maybe you've spent thousands or even tens of thousands of dollars on real estate books, videos, boot-camps and seminars, learning how to make money in real estate. Maybe you have your team in place—all the people you need to buy and manage property or to fix and flip for a profit. Maybe you are even an experienced real estate investor who has already flipped properties successfully, but now you are looking to take your business to the next level. Whatever your current situation is, you are primed and ready, eager and excited. You know that you have what it takes.

All you need is money.

You need the capital to propel your business plan forward. If you could just find someone with money to believe in you, to invest with you, you know in your heart that you could make substantial profits for both you and your money partner. Given the opportunity, you know you could prove that you have both the skills and integrity to create a profitable real estate investment business. But you don't know where that opportunity is.

Does this situation sound familiar?

Let's imagine for a moment what your life might look like, six months or a year from today, when a lack of capital is no longer an impediment to your real estate investment activities. What would that look like? What would that *feel* like?

Here is what I *know* it will look like. Every deal you do can be funded entirely with private money or OPM—Other People's Money. You'll be able to use OPM to fund:

- the purchase price
- all the closing costs and prepaid expenses
- the rehab costs
- all your holding costs
- your marketing costs

But wait—it gets better! Having access to a potentially unlimited supply of capital will allow you to:

- snap up every good deal you can lay your hands on;
- get cash discounts from highly motivated sellers;
- have your offers moved to the front of the line, ahead of others that rely on bank financing or seller carrybacks;
- close with blinding speed (which is music to a motivated seller's ears!); and
- never slow down your marketing efforts for fear of running out of money!

That is what's in store for you when you tap the growing and virtually unlimited capital resource known as private money.

What is private money? You probably already know, and that's why you are reading this book—to help you find it! But just to be clear about what we are talking about, private money is from private individuals *you* meet. Private money is not hard money, hedge fund money, brokered money or money from anyone in the business of lending money.

But whether or not you already know about private money, what you may not truly appreciate is just how huge and untapped this resource has become over the last decade.

The past ten years have been referred to by some as the "lost decade," because people have seen their retirement savings undergo an onslaught of losses, from the stock market, to the real estate crash, to paltry bond yields—not to mention the slow-growth market of nearly zero percent interest rates paid by banks on savings and CDs. The truth of the matter is that most investors are not just hungry for yields—they are starving for them.

Millions of people from the baby boomer generation (those born between 1946 and 1964) have been saving up for decades and are nearing retirement. Many of them are sitting on hundreds of thousands if not millions of dollars in cash and highly liquid assets. These people are looking to invest in assets that offer a higher yield. All told, retirement accounts in the United States alone are believed to account for over $20 trillion! And the sad truth is that most of these retirement-aged Americans are not on track financially to support the retirement lifestyle of their dreams.

What does this mean for you? It means that people with money are looking for opportunities to boost the yields that they are earning on their savings. They are looking to make up for lost time and lost returns.

They are looking for *you*.

You have the solution to their problem. *You* have the answer to their need to earn higher yields. *You* have the key that can help them *supercharge* their savings. You have the cure for that nightmare that keeps them up at nights—the fear of running out of money before they run out of life!

People *need* what you have to offer. They are looking for someone just like you who can show them how they can earn high yields, but with safety and security features in place that are not available in stocks and other investments. Your challenge is to find these people and show them that you have a plan that will help them achieve their financial goals and dreams.

This book will tell you how to attract private individuals looking for investment alternatives to disappointing stocks, bonds, CDs, and mutual funds. It will show you how to appeal to people who are looking for opportunities to wisely invest their capital for *real* growth and income. Real estate has historically been and still remains one of the best ways to accomplish both of those things. And you are the person who can make it happen.

The Private Money Guy

So who am I and why should you listen to me? I've been raising money for over thirty years, both debt and equity capital. Before I became a hard money loan broker, I worked for more than twenty years for a closely held real estate development company. In those years, I submitted loan applications to borrow on real estate hundreds of times—from banks, from insurance companies, and from hard money lenders. I have also helped to buy and sell dozens of commercial and residential properties, and I've raised equity capital for several joint-venture projects. I've been in the real estate business in some form or fashion for my entire life.

When the market took a nosedive in 2007 and the company I was part of didn't survive, I found myself in the position of thousands of other real estate investors—with no real estate, no capital, and no job. I had to start over. In the summer of 2008, I became a hard money loan broker. I knew that people were looking for money, and I figured I could help them find it.

I started Pacific Private Money from my home office. And in just three years, I went from zero investors and zero loans to $32 million in annual originations. By the end of my fourth year, I had originated over four hundred hard money loans and attracted hundreds of individual private lenders. Those private lenders were throwing their money at me faster than I could place it.

As of April 2014, I had personally raised over $150 million in private capital for my mortgage investments and was on track to raise millions more.

As a professional money lender and money broker, I've had a front-row seat to thousands of loan applications from rehabbers, contractors, and real estate investors. How I formulated my strategies and practices for effectively attracting private money came from the combination of:

- speaking with and reviewing loan applications and presentations from over a thousand real estate investors; and
- my continual efforts to grow a database of private lenders who were willing to fund those loans.

Attract Private Money

Attracting private capital boils down to these fundamental

activities:

- How you show up
- Where you show up
- What you say
- What you leave them with

I'm going to help you understand how to do these activities effectively by telling you what questions a private lender is going to want you to answer. The information I am going to share with you revolve around what some refer to as the "famous five questions." These are the five basic questions that you need to answer in the mind of your prospective private lender if you hope to have any chance of convincing that person to invest with you.

These five questions are crucial to the preparation and delivery of your presentation. When you answer them right, your prospective investors will believe that you are the person who can help them. Answer these questions to their satisfaction, and you will be on your way to attracting unlimited capital for your real estate investment business.

How to Read This Book

Unlike a lot of real estate books, *The Insider's Guide to Attracting Private Money* is concise and to the point. You won't find a lot of fluff and extraneous stories. I strongly recommend that you read this book all the way through to the end, then reread it again from the beginning and prepare a plan of action for yourself based on the strategies I have suggested.

One of my mentors, Darren Hardy of *Success Magazine*, suggests that one of the challenges entrepreneurs face today is that we read a lot, but we no longer *study*. This book is intended to provide you with a blueprint for success in attracting private lenders. One quick read will not do that for you. Read, reread, think, and go deep with this topic. The success you achieve will be in direct proportion to the extra effort you put into this endeavor. And it will all be worth it in the end.

Are you ready? Let's get started.

Setting the Stage

It's Not about You

I chose the title *The Insider's Guide to Attracting Private Money* for this book with purpose. I am a firm believer in the power of attraction, as opposed to promotion. What is the difference?

Promotion is about you. Attraction is about the other person.

One of the keys to forming a successful relationship with an investor is a sincere focus on what is in the best interest of your prospective partner. This is especially true in attracting private money. When you demonstrate that you have the best interest of your prospective money partner at heart, and that your goal is to help your private lender make a great return on his or her money without taking unnecessary risk, you become extremely attractive.

By focusing on the needs, goals, and concerns of your prospective money partner, you create a loyal client for life— one who will refer you to others who can also benefit from your good work.

This book approaches the challenge of attracting private money from the vantage point of your private money lender. What are his or her primary thoughts and concerns over the prospect of working with you? What important questions will he or she need answers to?

I have found that there are five basic questions that cover these concerns. These five questions we will study, then, are presented from the perspective of your future private money partner. I use these questions to formulate a strategy I call The Five Steps to Money Method™. They are:

1. What is the opportunity?
2. How much money do you need?
3. How much money can I make?
4. When do I get my money back?
5. What happens if you disappear?

Virtually every important aspect of an investment opportunity falls somewhere within these five questions. By clearly and completely answering each of them, you will attract millions of dollars in private capital. How do I know that? Because I personally know hundreds of real estate investors who have successfully implemented this strategy. And I have personally raised over $150 million in private capital for my mortgage investments by using this exact strategy.

In fact, as you can see, none of these questions relate specifically to real estate. The Five Steps to Money Method™ will work for raising capital in *any* endeavor. Every successful business plan must answer each and every one of these questions or it will not attract the interest of investors. In the ensuing chapters, we will investigate each of these five questions individually. We will also review the components you need to provide your potential investors with attractive answers to all five questions.

Before we get into the details, let's run through an overview of each of these concepts.

What is the opportunity?

"I'm in contract to purchase a 3-bedroom, 2-bath single family home in a popular middle-class neighborhood. The property hasn't been remodeled in years, and we're getting it at a great discount. Well-remodeled homes in this neighborhood are selling on average for $300 per square foot, and the average days-on-market period is less than thirty days."

That is an example of a simple and well-articulated description of an opportunity that could be delivered like a thirty-second elevator pitch at a networking event; one that is attended by people with money. It's short and to the point, and it demonstrates your knowledge of the market. But answering the "What is the opportunity?" question in the mind of your prospective private lender goes far beyond the specific deal. In developing your more complete answer to this first question, your lender is also going to want to know things such as:

- Who are you?
- What is your background?
- What is your real estate experience?
- Can I see examples of your previous work?
- How well did it go before?

Providing your detailed background and experience lays the foundation of your credibility, and answers the silent sub-question of *"Why should I listen to you?"*

How much money do you need?

Answering this question involves creating a detailed budget for the opportunity. You might also present more than one scenario for how your prospective money partner can be involved. There are many ways to structure the opportunity in a way that will convince the investor to participate.

- Is it a loan?
- Is it an equity investment?
- Will you be using other capital in addition to your private lender?
- Will you be using leverage?

While you don't want to over-complicate or overwhelm a prospective lender with too many choices, understanding that there are many ways to structure a deal will help you to adjust your parameters based on a specific lender's preferences and comfort level.

How much can I make?

How much you offer to pay your private lender will normally depend on a number of variables. One of those variables is whether you offer collateral in the form of a mortgage or deed of trust on the subject property, or if you offer an equity membership in an LLC that is formed to acquire the property. Will you be offering payment in the form of a loan (interest), will you be sharing the profit, or will you strike a balance between both? If you share the profit, what is the split? To answer this question completely, you should include both a best-case and worst-case scenario.

When do I get my money back?

If you are planning to buy, fix, and flip a property, then your exit strategy (how you will repay your private lender) is fairly straightforward. You will pay the individual back at the close of escrow when the property is sold. But what if you want your partner to invest in more than one project at a time, or to reinvest his or her profits from one project into another one? What if your plan is to acquire rental properties to hold long-term?

Part of your budget should include a timetable that, like your profit plan, has a best-case and worst-case scenario. Showing that you have considered that the unexpected might happen makes you look more professional. Also, keep in mind that it's always better to under-promise and over-deliver than the other way around.

What happens if you disappear?

While you do want to have a plan in place in the event that you get hit by a bus, the bigger point of this question is to address the concern about what happens if things go wrong. What are the risks? What safety and security features have you built into your model? What protections are you proposing to prevent or reduce the prospect of a loss to your investor's principal?

This is the area that many real estate investors either skip entirely or downplay, but addressing these issues up front actually makes you look professional and shows that you have both considered and planned for all possibilities. Optimism is important, but blind optimism can work against your goals.

The Big Picture

Now you are getting the picture of how The Five Steps to Money Method™ is the foundation of an effective presentation that will weave together your story, your opportunity, and your promise in a way that impresses investors, creates confidence, and attracts capital to you in a big way.

One more note before we continue. In this book I use the terms "private lender" and "private money partner" interchangeably. Either term references a private individual or individuals who make their money available to you, whether in the form of a loan, an equity investment, or both. I use the term "hard money lender" to mean a person or company that makes a loan to you and charges both interest and origination fees on it. Most hard money lenders have their own private lenders as their source of capital. The purpose of this book is to give you important strategies that will help you find and attract private money lenders of your own.

Let's now dive into the detailed strategies for answering each of the five questions in The Five Steps to Money Method™, beginning with the first one: "What is the opportunity?"

Question 1 — What Is the Opportunity?

Anonymity: Your Biggest Barrier to Success

I know dozens of talented contractors who have the skills to build beautiful homes, but they have trouble finding anyone to back them financially. I also know of hundreds of real estate investors and rehabbers who can do great work remodeling and flipping a home yet they can't seem to find a financial partner to help them take their business to the next level. Why do you think that is? The simple answer is because they have never put forth the time and effort to build a proper portfolio and credibility package. They haven't overcome the biggest barrier to success in business: anonymity.

Your answers to "What is the opportunity?" and its unspoken but very important counterpart, "Why should I listen to you?" are the foundation upon which you build the argument in favor of investing with you. These questions take you and your opportunity out of the shadows and show your potential investors exactly who and what they're dealing with, right up front.

"Why should I listen to you?" is a question that presents you with the opportunity to sell your prospective private lender on the merits of investing *in you*. This is where you put forth your best marketing skills to showcase who you are, what you know, what you've done, and what you plan to do next. You are handing your prospect an invitation to join you on an exciting journey of extraordinary returns on their investment, the likes of which he or she won't readily find anywhere else.

As I mentioned earlier, I've had a front-row seat to thousands of loan applications from rehabbers, contractors, and real estate investors. I've seen everything from newbie investors to massively experienced professionals flipping million-dollar remodels in San Francisco. The one thing they all had in common was that they had to impress upon me that they were individuals I could trust to do what they said they could do. That was what made me feel comfortable loaning them money.

How did they do it?

One of the most valuable investments of your time, energy, and creativity that you can make is in the development of your *credibility package*—the informational handout that will be an extremely effective fundraising tool for you. The trick is preparing it correctly. Your credibility package should contain items such as:

- an executive summary of the opportunity
- your biography
- your resume
- your experience, training, and education
- a spreadsheet showing your previous projects
- before and after pictures of one or more of your previous projects
- descriptions of your team members and their bios
- additional items

The simple truth is that people will only invest with you if you succeed in getting them to *know, like,* and *trust* you. This is extremely important. A well-prepared credibility package will help your potential investors to get to know you. Actually presenting it to them will give you an opportunity to get them to like you. And the thoroughness of your presentation will demonstrate a level of trustworthiness that the written package alone can never create.

Build Your Credibility Package

Words alone are almost never enough to get people to know, like, and trust you with their precious life savings. You've just seen why you need a strong credibility package. Now let's take a closer look at the credibility components I listed above.

Executive summary: An executive summary is a brief story of the type of investment opportunity you're offering in general. It is not specific to any one project. Rather, it's an overview of why, how, and what you are doing to create value in real estate. Your executive summary can be a bit boastful, as long as you support your claims and provide the necessary details to back them up.

Biography: Your biography, or bio, is not a resume. It focuses specifically on you and your accomplishments, experience, and expertise, and it can also be a bit boastful if it is done in taste. It is told like a story, and its purpose is to market you as an expert.

Resume: You might also include your resume as a separate item. Your resume lists the facts of your career and education. Between your bio and your resume, you should be able to highlight all of your relevant experience, education, and training. In fact, I have seen presentations from people who have taken so many different courses and trainings that they needed to highlight them all on a separate page. Look at it this way: if it's something you think an investor should know about you, it should be in your material.

Spreadsheet your experience: I've seen spreadsheets of previous projects from experienced flippers that listed information including addresses, purchase price, remodeling costs, date purchased and date sold, sales price, net profit, and even returns to their investors. All of this was nicely laid out in rows and columns. And yet when I suggest to certain clients that they should do the same thing, I sometimes hear things like, "What? That's confidential!" My response? Nonsense! My advice? If you have experience, leverage it! Success sells. The more transparent you are about your experience, the more attractive you will be to your prospect.

Before and after photos: Nothing tells the story of your ability to improve real estate better than strong pictures. In this business, it really is true that a picture is worth a thousand words. I have seen great examples of both interior and exterior before and after photos, all nicely laid out on one or more pages. You can do a lot with *Microsoft Word* or *Microsoft Publisher* to make your before and after photos look top-notch. If you don't have those programs or don't know how to use them effectively, find someone who does and ask for help. And if you don't know of anyone who can help, there are inexpensive online services that will organize and format a presentation for you.

Brag about your team: Don't forget to include information about your team in your credibility package. Your team may include your contractor, designer, architect, stager, real estate agent, insurance agent, and attorney. If you are the contractor, list your sub-contractors. Include pictures of your team in the write-up.

Additional items: What else could you include in your credibility package? A picture of you and your family may make you look more approachable to a potential investor. If you have good credit, leverage it by including your credit report. Awards and affiliations are also a good idea. These additional items are especially important to include if you don't yet have experience or previous projects that you can promote.

Examples of and templates for an entire credibility package are included in my video training program, The Insider's Guide to Attracting Private Money™, available at www.AttractingPrivateMoney.com.

What If I Have No Experience?

For those of you without experience or previous projects, include the successes of your team members in your credibility package, instead. Leverage their talent and experience. If you are working with a coach, leverage that individual's success and experience. Contrary to popular belief, you don't need to have direct experience in order to attract capital!

An entrepreneur knows how to solve problems by leveraging other people's skills and talents. There are investors out there who understand this. You don't need to run the day-to-day operation. Now, if you bill yourself as the person who will find it, fix it, and flip it, you'd better be the one who does all of those things. Don't represent yourself by saying that you can do things if you can't.

Now you understand how to build a credibility package that sells you as a real estate investor. Now you have to sell the specific opportunity at hand. In the next chapter, I'll show you how to create the opportunity portion of your presentation by answering the second question in The Five Steps to Money Method™: "How much money do you need?"

Question 2 — How Much Money Do You Need?

An Opportunity to Believe In

How important is this question in the bigger scheme of The Five Steps to Money Method™? If you carry out the suggestions in this chapter correctly, investors will flock to you. But if you make a mistake, they may never return your call.

Your credibility package is the foundation that makes you a trustworthy individual. But the foundation that lends credibility to your opportunity itself in the eyes of your prospective private lender is an accurate, complete, and well-designed spreadsheet.

Creating a spreadsheet that is both complete and well-designed is tricky. You want your audience to be able to read and understand your numbers quickly and easily. Yet you also want your spreadsheet, which is a numerical representation of *everything* about your project from start to finish, to be so complete that it does not leave out any significant cost item. In this chapter, I will show you how to strike that balance.

Spreadsheet for Success

Your initial opportunity package for your private lender should be a simplified summary of the whole transaction. When your private lender looks at it, that individual should clearly see what the expected costs are for the project and how you propose to capitalize on the available opportunity.

If you have taken any reputable course on real estate investing, it probably provided you with a spreadsheet template to help you determine how much to offer on a property. Do *not* use that template for your presentation spreadsheet because it may be too detailed. While the templates you receive in seminars are great tools for finding and analyzing opportunities, they are not the spreadsheets you want to show to your prospective private lender—at least not initially. Your investor may want to see your detailed assumptions later in the conversation, but the initial introduction to the opportunity must be simple and easy to understand.

That said, your summary should still be based on a detailed budget of all your cost items. As a lender, I have seen plenty of spreadsheets for proposed projects, and I can tell you that nothing hurts a loan application more than a spreadsheet that is clearly missing key cost components and that misrepresents (overstates) the true profit potential of a project.

Every spreadsheet representation of a proposed project must include all of the following major cost categories:

- acquisition costs
- rehab costs
- holding costs
- financing costs
- marketing costs
- sales costs

Acquisition costs: The total acquisition costs are always greater than the purchase price. The closing costs that you typically pay through escrow include the buyer's share of closing costs, such as title and escrow fees, among other things. These can amount to several thousands of dollars depending on various factors, such as customary procedures in the county where the project is located and the split of closing costs between buyer and seller, which may have been negotiated as part of your purchase offer.

Rehab budget: Your rehab budget should include all of your hard costs (materials and labor) as well as soft costs (insurance, architects, designers, permits). You should always include a contingency amount for unexpected yet typical cost overruns.

Holding, financing, and marketing costs: Holding costs include utilities and property taxes. If you decide to use a hard money purchase loan (a combination of debt and equity), then you will also have origination fees, junk fees, and interest carrying costs. Your marketing costs might include items like staging, advertising, and flyers.

Sales costs: Then of course there are all the costs of selling the finished project. Too many spreadsheets underestimate the typical costs of the sales transaction to the seller. Sales costs include city and county transfer taxes, any buyer credits that are typically offered, title insurance, escrow fees, and of course real estate commissions. Sales costs will typically amount to 8–10 percent of the sales price, yet I regularly see spreadsheet estimates that only show a 5–6 percent real estate commission. Make sure your numbers are accurate.

I have ready-to-use spreadsheet templates that you can use to jumpstart this component. With these templates, all you need to do is drop in the specific numbers of your deal and it's ready to go. These templates are included in my video training program, The Insider's Guide to Attracting Private Money™, available at www.AttractingPrivateMoney.com.

Keep It Simple

Your job and your goal is to make a handsome profit for your private lender. That's why you need to create the spreadsheet so that it clearly highlights how much your private lender can make with his or her investment. You can do this by creating a simplified summary page.

Your summary page recaps all of the detailed components in your spreadsheet so that you can present the proposed project on one page. Many people skip the summary page and just try to list every cost item on a single spreadsheet instead. However, that approach can be overwhelming for your private lenders to understand. You don't want to embarrass your prospective lender with complex spreadsheets, as they may not want to admit that they don't understand what they are looking at.

The best way to create an effective spreadsheet presentation is to use a multi-page spreadsheet. Page one is the summary page. The summary page shows the lender your estimate for the six cost categories we just covered, representing each with a single summary number. The details of the different component items are shown on the ensuing pages. Start a new page for each category. For example, you will want to use a separate page for the line-item breakdown of your detailed rehab budget.

The single most important item to show on the summary page of your proposed project is the profit component that you are offering to your prospective lender. Make sure that the bottom of the summary spreadsheet on page one presents the total projected gross profit that will be earned after the property is sold.

The very next line item after the profit number should be how much you propose to pay your private lender. *Your private lender is always paid first*. Remember, this is about your lender, not you. Highlight the amount you are offering to pay your lender in bold font. Show it both as a dollar amount and as the percentage return on the capital invested. If you expect to pay your lender back in, say, six months, you should also show the percentage return on his or her investment on an annualized basis.

Downplay the amount of profit that goes to you. You get what's left over, after your private lender has been handsomely rewarded.

Your simplified opportunity summary page, with a detailed spreadsheet attached to support it, is key to attracting private money. The next question in The Five Steps to Money Method™ is "How much can I make?" I'll show you how to determine how much you should offer to pay your private lender in the next chapter.

Question 3 — How Much Can I Make?

Happy Private Lender, Big Profits

Your job is to provide your private lender with fabulous returns. Do this, and you will have a loyal client for life. But exactly how do you determine how much to offer your private money lender? Are there rules of thumb or accepted norms for structuring your compensation offer?

First and foremost, there are no set rules in private lending. Compensation is whatever you and your money partner agree to—or, put another way, whatever you can convince someone to agree to.

That being said, the point of this book is to attract private money, and you are going to attract more private money if your compensation offers are competitive. My suggestion is to investigate your marketplace and find out whether there are accepted or expected norms regarding investor returns.

For example, in my marketplace—the San Francisco Bay Area—typical interest rates paid to private lenders on loans are among the lowest in the nation. As the real estate market recovered from the financial crisis, "flipper loans" priced at 10 percent were not uncommon. In other parts of the country, 12, 14 or even 18 percent might be the average rate of return paid to private lenders on short-term flipper loans.

But what about the compensation structures you can use that go beyond a simple loan? Let's take a look at the four primary compensation options available for you to offer to your prospective lender.

Pay Your Private Lender

The four major compensation options that you can offer your private lender are:

1. Profit split
2. Guaranteed interest
3. Lender points
4. Exit fees

1. Profit split

A profit split is a simple percentage split between you and your money partner. This compensation agreement is also known as a "joint venture." In the beginning, this is where many real estate investors start out with their money partners. It is generally—but not always—the most expensive form of private money lending.

Many of you are probably already familiar with the idea of a 50–50 split of profits, which is generally considered to be a typical and fair arrangement—a trade of *talent* for *capital*. The joint-venture model is the ultimate capitalist endeavor. "I have the time and talent; you have the capital. Let's joint venture on a deal and we'll both win big. We'll split the profits, right down the middle."

Well, in reality, there is nothing standard at all about joint venturing. As I stated earlier, the amount of compensation you offer to your private lender is whatever you and he or she can agree upon.

When my dad did one of his first equity joint ventures back in the early 1980s, he met a wealthy investor who agreed to put up the cash to build a project. Now, this was a commercial deal with big profit potential, and my dad, in order to get his foot in the door with this newfound partner, offered him a 75–25 percent profit split. That's right—75 percent of the profit went to his capital partner!

Is that a lot? Well, on the next two projects with this same investor, the split was 60 percent, 40 percent. And then, finally, after three successful projects together, it became a 50–50 split thereafter. So, was that first 75–25 split a bad deal for my dad? Not if you look at the relationship that it created and the end result—a relationship that my dad ended up making a ton of money from over the ensuing ten-year period.

With joint ventures, oftentimes the agreement will include not only an agreed profit split, but also a provision for a "preferred" rate of interest. Preferred interest means that the first part of the profit goes to the private lender. The private lender therefore gets preference.

This means that even if the profit on the deal turns out to be skinny—in other words, significantly less than you projected—your investor receives the greater of:

1. the agreed upon split, (i.e. 50–50); or
2. interest on his or her capital investment, calculated at the preferred rate.

So if, by calculating what your investor would have earned using the preferred interest rate, you come up with a number that is greater than a 50 percent share of the profits from your project, then your lender gets the preferred return—the greater number—and you get what's left.

Why offer a preferred rate of return to your investor?

Because offering a preferred rate of return is a great way to demonstrate your credibility and integrity. It's your promise to your lender that you know what you are doing. Competency starts with standing by your numbers and your work. When you do this, you are telling your lender that you are so confident in your numbers that you will essentially work for free if you are wrong.

In the industry, a preferred rate of return is referred to as "the pref." So if you offer someone a 50–50 split of the profits and that person asks if you are offering a "pref," that's what your prospective investor is talking about. And in my opinion, your answer to that question should always be "Yes."

A common "pref" that I often see is 12 percent. That translates into a 12 percent annualized preferred return on the money that your partner contributes. Remember, however, that a preferred return is *not* a guaranteed return. In other words, if there is no profit or only a little profit, that little profit goes to the investor even if it doesn't add up to a 12 percent annualized return. The investor gets his or her piece of the profits first, but if those profits just aren't there, you are not expected to make up the shortfall.

2. Guaranteed interest

Guaranteed interest is essentially a straight loan, and it is often the most economical form of private investor capital. Using the "loan" format is most common when you have your own capital to contribute to the project.

If your lender is putting up all the cash for your project, then it's more likely that you will use a joint-venture model for compensation. However, even though it's more difficult to get someone to loan you 100 percent of the project costs, it's certainly not impossible. You are simply more likely to use the loan model when you find a money partner who is willing to lend you perhaps 70–90 percent of the total project budget, with your money going in first.

You sell the concept of arranging, say, an 80 percent project loan by showing your investor the effective exposure of his or her loan as it relates to your projected after repair value (ARV), also known as future value. In other words, the loan might be equal to 80 percent of the project's budget, but it may really only be equal to 65 percent of the future value after you have done the remodel. One way to demonstrate this is to run a report of recent comparable sales to support your projected resale value. Another way is to obtain a future value appraisal.

The lower the percentage of the loan as it relates to the total budget, the lower the interest rate you should offer to your lender. Conversely, the higher the percentage, the more interest you should be offering. If you are seeking 90–95 or even 100 percent of the project costs in the form of a loan, you should expect to offer the lender a return commensurate with that risk, and 12–18 percent wouldn't be out of line in that case, depending on your market.

Unless your lender specifically requests monthly interest payments, your offer should be to allow the interest to accrue and then to pay it to the investor along with the loan principal all at once, upon sale of the property. That way, you don't have to supply monthly interest payments out of pocket while you are remodeling and selling the property.

3. Lender points

Lender points, which are equal to 1 percent of the loan amount per point, are a great way to spice up the return for your lender. I've seen many people persuade lenders who were "on the fence" to agree to their projects by throwing lender points into the deal.

When you borrow from a hard money broker, you will almost always pay those points up front, which really means that they get deducted from the loan proceeds. Your private lender probably doesn't need up-front points. However, if you offer your money partner one or more lender points in addition to the interest rate, payable on the back end when you sell the property, then that can be a creative way to get your investor to loan you the money instead of having to split the profits with him or her.

4. Exit fees

Finally, we have the fourth and final way of compensating your investor: exit fees.

Exit fees are always paid at the end of the transaction, when the property sells (hence the use of "exit" in the term "exit fees"). Exit fees can be a percentage on the loan amount, paid on the back end, like lender points. Exit fees are another creative way to compel a prospective private lender to invest with you. They are typically offered in addition to a guaranteed rate of interest.

I've seen exit fees as high as twenty-five points. That's 25 percent of the loan amount, as an extra fee, in *addition* to the interest rate, all paid when the project sells. Whether or not something like this is a better deal for you than a 50–50 split of the profits depends on how good the deal looks. Sometimes an opportunity looks just too good to split 50–50, but if you offer an aggressive exit fee, the investor feels like he or she can't lose.

Another way to structure the exit fee is to base it on the sale price, much like a real estate agent's commission. You might offer your lender a fee that is equal to 5 percent of the sale price as an exit fee on that individual's loan, in addition to the interest rate. Again, this is a very good way to entice someone to make an aggressive loan.

Exit fees are a creative way to attract capital for your projects, and the different ways you can structure the offer in order to create a win for both you and your lender are limited only by your imagination.

One final benefit of the exit-fee model is that the math is much easier to work out than it is with a profit-sharing agreement. So if you like to keep things simple, the exit-fee model may be the way to go.

I give you free sample agreements that illustrate these four options in my comprehensive video training program, The Insider's Guide to Attracting Private Money™, available at www.AttractingPrivateMoney.com.

Using Leverage

I'll say it again: your job is to work hard to help make your money partner a fabulous return on his or her investment. For that, you will also be handsomely rewarded.

One way to accomplish this goal is through the prudent use of leverage. Using leverage will typically boost the yield your investor receives, because you will be using borrowed money in addition to your investor's money. In other words, instead of having your investor put up all the funds, you can use a hard money loan for a portion of the budget, and your money partner's capital for the balance.

Working with a reputable hard money broker can have other benefits as well. They may be able to help you draft security documents between you and your investor. The backing of the hard money lender also provides third-party verification of the viability of your project.

Using a hard money loan may eat into your overall profits to some extent, but as a general rule, you will see that the return to your investor is significantly higher when you bring a hard money lender into the equation than it is when you do an all-cash deal. In other words, your personal profit share will be less due to your share of the loan interest and fees, but because your private lender is putting up far less money, the mathematical return on his investment is increased, often significantly, by the use of leverage.

There are no set rules when it comes to deciding how to pay your private lender. The only limit is your own creativity. In the next chapter, I'll show you how to create confidence with your investor by determining how you will repay your lender's money.

Question 4 — When Do I Get My Money Back?

The Lender Comes First

The key point in any conversation with a prospective lender is this: the lender always gets paid first, no matter what, before you ever see a dime of profit.

This is a cardinal rule that must never be broken. Consider it your fiduciary responsibility as a serious real estate investor to protect and safeguard the capital of your investor at all times. Promise your lender that he or she will always get paid first, and keep that promise. Every decision you make should always be in the best interest of your money partner. Always.

The fourth question in The Five Steps to Money Method™ is "When do I get my money back?" Answer this question correctly, and you will create a loyal client. That loyal client will tell his or her friends. And you will become very wealthy.

The Exit Strategy

Paying back your lender is all about your exit strategy. On a fix-and-flip project, the exit strategy for your money partner is straightforward: you pay back the investor's capital investment plus his or her share of interest or profits at the close of escrow, when the property sells.

The key here is creating confidence in the mind of your lender. Your money partner needs to know that he or she can count on you to hold up your end of the deal. In this chapter, we'll look at a few different strategies to help you show your private lender that you can be trusted to pay back what you owe.

Offer Security

One way to reassure your investor is to offer to secure his or her capital contribution by recording a mortgage against the property. This way, your private lender knows that he or she will get paid from the proceeds of the sale, directly from escrow. That eliminates the question "What if you decide to run off to Mexico with my money?"

Recording your investor's capital investment in the form of a mortgage or deed of trust against the property gives the lender the ability to control the distribution of proceeds from the sale through the power of reconveyance. This means that money cannot be paid from sale proceeds until the lender releases his or her mortgage interest in the property first. Of course, if the money is being contributed in the form of a loan, you should be recording the lender's collateral security as a mortgage anyway. But if the compensation arrangement is a joint-venture profit share, this additional offer of security may be what it takes to get your first deal approved.

Set Time Frames

Always try to use realistic time frames in estimating when your private lender will get his or her money back. Don't say it will be ninety days when it is more likely to be six months. Don't say six months if it's a significant remodel that probably won't sell for nine to twelve months. Under-promise and over-deliver—never the opposite.

Buy-and-Hold Strategies

What if you are raising money to buy and hold property for rental income, and offering attractive mid- to long-term fixed yields? What is your exit strategy then?

Many real estate investors promise to pay their private lender back in two to three years through a conventional bank refinance arrangement. However, be careful using that as your only exit strategy. I know investors who created portfolios of rental properties using private money, only to find that they were unable to obtain conventional loans years later.

Bank loans are much harder to come by these days thanks to all the new regulations passed in the wake of the Dodd-Frank finance reforms. So have a Plan B (and C) in the event that the banks turn down your refinance applications.

Sell Your Lender's Note

If bank financing is not available, an additional strategy to put in your plan could be an offer to help sell your lender's note on the open market at full price, at no cost to them—including fees. There is a vibrant secondary marketplace for high-interest, performing notes, and you can often sell these notes at no discount to the seller.

In other words, even though there are investors out there who are looking to buy notes at a discount—such as paying $90,000 for a $100,000 note—you can also find internet-based marketplaces where you can sell high-yielding, performing notes at full price. Selling a note at full price is referred to as selling the note "at par value."

Get a Hard Money Loan

A third strategy you can use is to obtain a hard money loan in order to retire your money partner's loan at maturity. This will cost you points and fees. However, assuming that the value of the property has increased, you should be able to refinance your partner's loan with a larger loan that includes the loan fees, thus requiring no money out of your pocket.

Have Multiple Exit Strategies

Multiple exit strategies are always the best way to go. An impressive repayment strategy that you could write into your "buy and hold" loan offering proposal might look something like this:

1. I will repay your loan through conventional bank financing at maturity; or
2. Upon mutual agreement, you extend the term of the loan for X years; or
3. I will assist you in selling your note at no costs or fees; or
4. I will obtain a new hard money loan to retire your loan; or
5. I will sell the property and repay your loan.

That's five different strategies you have listed to repay your private lender's loan. When you write that into your business plan, there is no question that you have thought through all of the available options to return the lender's money, as agreed.

One of the keys to working with private money lenders is understanding that, in general, private lenders don't want to get their money back too fast, nor do they want to make long-term commitments. Term preferences of private lenders will typically range anywhere from six months to five years. Find out your prospective lender's preference regarding time frames up front. Shorter term lenders are better for fix-and-flip projects, and three- to five-year lenders are better for buy-and-hold strategies.

Having multiple exit strategies built into your business plan makes you look like a pro and gives your lender the added comfort of knowing that he or she won't be stuck in the loan forever. From here, I'll walk you through an important part of your presentation that most real estate investors leave out: disclosing risk.

Question 5 — What Happens If You Disappear?

The Advantage of Disclosing Risk

You need to disclose the risk involved in your project for one simple reason. That reason is that you are asking people to lend you a portion of their life savings, and they are entitled to know what happens to that money in the event that you exit the picture.

The fifth question we answer in The Five Steps to Money Method™, "What happens if you disappear?" is asking much more than just "What happens if you get hit by a bus?" Disclosing risk is a very important yet often overlooked or ignored piece of the private lending equation.

That is, risk disclosure is often overlooked or ignored by borrowers. Your prospective private lender, on the other hand, is absolutely thinking about the risks of investing with you whether you bring them up or not. And what that prospective lender wants to hear from you is, "What are the risks, and what are your plans if things go wrong?"

You can answer this question by showing your lender how you are structuring your company and what measures you are taking to protect that individual's investment. For example, who on your team is positioned to take over in the event that something happens to you? If you can address this question and others like it, you will show your potential lender that you have thought this through, and that you take the protection of his or her capital investment very seriously.

The level of detail that you go into when disclosing risk is up to you (with sound advice from your real estate attorney). But the most basic risk disclosure essentially boils down to this message:

Your investor could lose some or all of his or her money.

That is why disclosing risk is such an important factor when you create your credibility and opportunity presentation.

Disclosures

Addressing and disclosing risks in your write-up and presentation will make you look professional and thorough, just as the other important components that we have discussed so far in this book have done.

Many real estate investors don't want to include risk-factor disclosures in their credibility and opportunity packages because they are afraid that they will scare away their prospective private lenders. They worry that if their potential lender understood the risks, then that person would decide not to invest with them.

However, just sitting back and hoping that everything goes perfectly all the time is not a strong strategy for success. The truth is that many real estate entrepreneurs have ended up in lawsuits because they failed to provide even the most basic disclosure of potential risks.

I am not an attorney, and this does not constitute legal advice. You should *strongly* consider engaging a real estate attorney to advise you if you plan to raise capital from private individuals. That being said, I have attended numerous real estate conferences and seminars on the topic of private capital, and I have seen many examples of risk disclosures ranging from simple ones to explanations that were long and complicated. As an example, for my mortgage pool fund, I provide prospective investors with a memorandum that includes over twenty pages of risk-factor disclosures.

The fact is that there are basic risks that you should be disclosing to your investors. That disclosure should be included in any write-up you create for the purpose of raising capital from private individuals.

You don't disclose these risks to your potential investor to scare them away. You disclose them so that the investor can make an informed decision. Risk factors you might discuss could include things such as:

- changes in the real estate market
- cash flow problems
- conflicts of interest
- an unproven real estate investing company (if you've never done a deal before)

Changes in the real estate market

Your opportunity presentation is based on a set of assumptions. Those assumptions include things like market demand, potential market appreciation, and an estimate of the increase in value as a result of your planned improvements.

However, the real estate market is subject to cycles that can affect the marketability, pricing, and days-on-market estimate of your project. Real estate can and does decline in value as a result of certain market forces. Rising interest rates, job growth, joblessness, new inventory, and other factors can contribute to a drop in demand and prices for real estate in a given market. Your prediction of how well your proposed project will do should be based on a careful review of local market conditions, but you cannot guarantee that the results you predict will be realized.

Cash flow problems

You have proposed a budget and a spreadsheet to your lender that shows your sources and uses of funds. But what if you come across significant and unexpected cost increases? Do you have the ability to cover them? Typically, your money partner will not be under any obligation to fund additional costs beyond the agreed-upon budget unless you bring this up in your written agreement beforehand. If the project stops as a result of running out of cash, you could be faced with mounting costs and declining profits as time goes on.

Conflicts of interest

Are you planning to dedicate 100 percent of your time to this one project with your prospective money partner? Or do you have other projects or work obligations that might be construed as "conflicts of interest"? You can make a statement in your presentation that gives your lender notice that, while you are dedicated to the success of this endeavor, you are nonetheless free to pursue other business ventures or obligations, as well.

Unproven real estate investing company

If you are new to real estate investing or if you have formed a new company to pursue real estate investments, you may not have a track record of success. In that case, your business model is unproven.

Changes in the market, cash flow problems, conflicts of interest, and an unproven real estate company are just a few examples of the risks that you may want to disclose to your lender. There are many others that you can identify and include in your proposal to give your investor a complete picture of what the project will entail. A qualified real estate attorney is an integral component to your team and should be consulted to assist you in drafting an appropriate disclosure statement.

Protect Yourself

Although I have been telling you to always put the best interests of your private lender first, the fact of the matter is that the primary purpose of your disclosure statement is to protect *you* in case your lender chooses to sue you. If you can demonstrate that you disclosed material risks to your private lender *before* that individual invested with you, you will be much better protected in a court of law.

In order to be up front with potential investors, be sure to disclose everything that you would disclose to your own grandmother, if she were to invest with you.

A more detailed discussion of disclosures, including sample disclosure statements, can be found in my comprehensive video training program, The Insider's Guide to Attracting Private Money™, available at www.AttractingPrivateMoney.com.

Access the World of Private Money

Beyond The Five Steps to Money Method™

The Five Steps to Money Method™ covers the essential elements that every credibility and opportunity package must contain in order to be effective at attracting private money.

At the beginning of this book, I suggested that attracting private money boiled down to four fundamental activities:

1. How you show up
2. Where you show up
3. What you say
4. What you leave them with

I've shown you my secrets to attracting private money using The Five Steps to Money Method™. This will get you started attracting fast, unlimited capital, so you can build real estate wealth. I am confident that as you implement these new techniques, you will find private investors to fund your deals.

While The Five Steps to Money Method™ covers many of the four fundamental activities listed above and is the foundation for your fundraising undertakings, it is only the beginning. There are more elements and strategies to attracting private money that have not been covered here.

For example, the most common question I get is "Where do I *go* to find my own private lenders?" I wrote this book because when I hear that question, more often than not those people *aren't yet ready to meet potential private lenders*. They have not done their homework. They have not prepared the strong credibility and opportunity packages that are so crucial to making them look like a professional who is ready to work with private lenders.

Preparation is a key first step. Networking for private lenders without the proper tools in hand is like fishing without bait. You only get one chance to make a first impression. Imagine showing up at a real estate event and meeting a potential lender, only to realize that you have nothing to demonstrate to that person that you are not just another wanna-be real estate investor with no plan, no vision, and no credibility. In other words, you look just like most people who are "trying to do something in real estate."

If you do the things I have suggested in this book correctly, you will put yourself in the top 5 percent of all real estate investors in terms of planning and preparation.

But where do you go once you have created your presentation? How do you meet prospective private lenders? What's the first thing you should say? Once you have laid the groundwork and created your credibility and opportunity packages—then what?

Here's the good news.

I've created a program that dives deeply into *all* of the key areas of *finding, attracting, and landing private lenders*. It contains all of my secrets. All of the things I have learned along the way to attracting hundreds of private lenders of my own. All of the things that I tried; what worked, and what didn't. I even explore the areas covered in this book in much greater depth, giving you more indispensable information about the crucial elements of attracting private lenders.

The Insider's Guide to Attracting Private Money™ video training program includes all of this, plus a bonus section filled with sample files including visual examples of great credibility-package components from real clients who have successfully attracted their own private lenders. There are templates of credibility and opportunity packages that will jump-start you on your way to finding and attracting private lenders. All of my best ideas and proven strategies are here, pulled together into one comprehensive program.

You will learn:

- All of the different ways to find private lenders, which ones work best, and which ones are a waste of your time.
- Where to go to find people with money to invest.
- The behavioral and personality traits that are more effective in attracting people with capital to invest.
- How to create a masterful credibility package that will "shock and awe" potential lenders.
- The effective networking techniques that have worked wonders for my capital-raising endeavors.
- The different types of private lenders and how to work best with each of them.
- The elements of a private money lender disclosure statement.
- The secrets to working with hard money lenders to grow your real estate business more quickly.
- Proven marketing concepts that will make your materials stand out from the pack.
- Plus my own personal development tips and time-management strategies that I picked up from some of

the most famous and successful thought leaders today (and which I spent tens of thousands of dollars to learn!).

Are you ready to take your business to the next level? Are you ready to make your real estate investment activities the envy of your peers?

I am grateful for the opportunity to share these secrets with you and look forward to hearing back from you as you achieve success in attracting private money. Please log on to our website (www.AttractingPrivateMoney.com) and send comments, feedback, and suggestions our way. Let us know about your success.

Visit my website at www.AttractingPrivateMoney.com to jump-start your way to finding, attracting, and landing private lenders—and to start accessing the unlimited capital resource known as private money.

GET YOUR

ATTRACTING PRIVATE MONEY

BONUS!

Exclusive Interview
with Mark Hanf

- Available only to book buyers!
- Discover how to find investors who want to
  invest their money with you!
- Learn about credibility packages and how to
  leverage them to close new deals

3 WAYS TO GET THIS!

BY WEB: Visit www.AttractingPrivateMoneyBook.com/bonus
BY TEXT: Text your name and email to (415) 779-7276.
BY PHONE: Call (415) 779-7276 and leave your name and email

(Standard message and data rates apply. Text HELP for help and STOP to quit)

About the Author

Insider's Guide to Attracting Private Money is written by industry insider Mark Hanf, broker and president of Pacific Private Money, Inc. Pacific Private Money, Inc. is one of the fastest-growing hard money loan brokerages in Northern California. The company originated over $150 million in loans in the last few years, many of them "fix & flip" loans to rehabbers and flippers.

Having uncovered the secret to gaining access to unlimited private capital, Mark attracted hundreds of private investors to his lending practice and is now known as the "Private Money Guy." He is a regular speaker at real estate events and clubs throughout California, and is a member of the American Association of Private Money Lenders (AAPL) and the California Mortgage Association (CMA).

Mark is co-host of a popular San Francisco Bay Area weekly 1-hour real estate radio show on 910 AM KKSF, *"The Best of Investing"*. He was asked by a leading real estate training organization to conduct a two-day boot camp and six-week mastermind coaching program on Attracting Private Money. The enthusiastic marketplace reception towards these events was a significant part of the inspiration for this book and accompanying educational video series, The Insider's Guide to Attracting Private Money Video Training Program, available at www.AttractingPrivateMoney.com.